Key Facts™ on the Philippines

~Essential Information on the Philippines~

By Patrick W. Nee

The Internationalist®
www.internationalist.com

The Internationalist®

International Business, Investment, and Travel

Published by:

The Internationalist Publishing Company

96 Walter Street/ Suite 200

Boston, MA 02131, USA

Tel: 617-354-7722

www.internationalist.com

PN@internationalist.com

Copyright © 2013 by PWN

The Internationalist is a Registered Trademark. "Key Facts" and "The Internationalist Business Guides" are Trademarks of The Internationalist Publishing Company.

All Rights are reserved under International, Pan-American, and Pan-Asian Conventions. No part of this book may be reproduced in any form without the written permission of the publisher. All rights vigorously enforced

Table Of Contents

Chapter 1: Background

Chapter 2: People and Society

Chapter 3: Government and Key Leaders

Chapter 4: Military

Chapter 5: Geography

Chapter 6: Economy

Chapter 7: Energy

Chapter 8: Communications

Chapter 9: Transportation

Chapter 10: Transnational Issues

Map of the Philippines

Chapter 1: Background

The Philippine Islands became a Spanish colony during the 16th century; they were ceded to the US in 1898 following the Spanish-American War. In 1935 the Philippines became a self-governing commonwealth. Manuel QUEZON was elected president and was tasked with preparing the country for independence after a 10-year transition. In 1942 the islands fell under Japanese occupation during World War II, and US forces and Filipinos fought together during 1944-45 to regain control. On 4 July 1946 the Republic of the Philippines attained its independence. A 20-year rule by Ferdinand MARCOS ended in 1986, when a "people power" movement in Manila ("EDSA 1") forced him into exile and installed Corazon AQUINO as president. Her presidency was hampered by several coup attempts that prevented a return to full political stability and economic development. Fidel RAMOS was elected president in 1992. His administration was marked by increased stability and by progress on economic reforms. In 1992, the US closed its last military bases on the islands. Joseph ESTRADA was elected president in 1998. He was succeeded by his vice-president, Gloria MACAPAGAL-ARROYO, in January 2001 after ESTRADA's stormy impeachment trial on corruption charges broke down and another "people power" movement ("EDSA 2") demanded his resignation. MACAPAGAL-ARROYO was elected to a six-year term as president in May 2004. Her presidency was marred by several corruption allegations but the Philippine economy was one of the few to avoid contraction following the 2008 global financial crisis, expanding each year of her administration. Benigno AQUINO III was elected to a six-year term as president in May 2010. The Philippine Government faces threats from several groups, some of which are on the US Government's Foreign Terrorist Organization list. Manila has waged a decades-long struggle against ethnic Moro insurgencies in the southern Philippines, which has led to a peace accord with the Moro National Liberation Front and ongoing peace talks with the Moro Islamic Liberation Front. The decades-long Maoist-inspired New People's Army insurgency also operates through much of the country. The Philippines faces increased tension with China over disputed territorial and maritime claims in the South China Sea.

Chapter 2: People and Society

Nationality:
　　noun: Filipino(s)
　　adjective: Philippine

Ethnic groups:
　　Tagalog 28.1%, Cebuano 13.1%, Ilocano 9%, Bisaya/Binisaya 7.6%, Hiligaynon Ilonggo 7.5%, Bikol 6%, Waray 3.4%, other 25.3% (2000 census)

Languages:
　　Filipino (official; based on Tagalog) and English (official); eight major dialects - Tagalog, Cebuano, Ilocano, Hiligaynon or Ilonggo, Bicol, Waray, Pampango, and Pangasinan

Religions:
　　Catholic 82.9% (Roman Catholic 80.9%, Aglipayan 2%), Muslim 5%, Evangelical 2.8%, Iglesia ni Kristo 2.3%, other Christian 4.5%, other 1.8%, unspecified 0.6%, none 0.1% (2000 census)

Population:
　　105,720,644 (July 2013 est.)
　　country comparison to the world: 12

Age structure:
　　0-14 years: 34% (male 18,339,398/female 17,607,472)

<u>15-24 years</u>: 19.1% (male 10,259,385/female 9,896,090)

<u>25-54 years</u>: 36.8% (male 19,550,257/female 19,369,177)

<u>55-64 years</u>: 5.7% (male 2,772,003/female 3,239,659)

<u>65 years and over</u>: 4.4% (male 2,023,118/female 2,664,085) (2013 est.)

Median age:

<u>total</u>: 23.3 years

<u>male</u>: 22.8 years

<u>female</u>: 23.8 years (2013 est.)

Population growth rate:

1.84% (2013 est.)

<u>country comparison to the world</u>: 63

Birth rate:

24.62 births/1,000 population (2013 est.)

<u>country comparison to the world</u>: 59

Death rate:

4.95 deaths/1,000 population (2013 est.)

<u>country comparison to the world</u>: 185

Net migration rate:

-1.25 migrant(s)/1,000 population (2013 est.)

<u>country comparison to the world</u>: 152

Urbanization:

urban population: 48.8% of total population (2011)

rate of urbanization: 2.16% annual rate of change (2010-15 est.)

Major urban areas - population:

MANILA (capital) 11.449 million; Davao 1.48 million; Cebu City 845,000; Zamboanga 827,000 (2009)

Sex ratio:

at birth: 1.05 male(s)/female

0-14 years: 1.04 male(s)/female

15-24 years: 1.04 male(s)/female

25-54 years: 1.01 male(s)/female

55-64 years: 0.86 male(s)/female

65 years and over: 0.76 male(s)/female

total population: 1 male(s)/female (2013 est.)

Maternal mortality rate:

99 deaths/100,000 live births (2010)

country comparison to the world: 73

Infant mortality rate:

total: 18.19 deaths/1,000 live births

country comparison to the world: 99

male: 20.59 deaths/1,000 live births

female: 15.66 deaths/1,000 live births (2013 est.)

Life expectancy at birth:

total population: 72.21 years
country comparison to the world: 135
male: 69.26 years
female: 75.31 years (2013 est.)

Total fertility rate:

3.1 children born/woman (2013 est.)
country comparison to the world: 53

Contraceptive prevalence rate:

48.9% (2011)

Health expenditures:

3.6% of GDP (2010)
country comparison to the world: 174

Physicians density:

1.15 physicians/1,000 population (2004)

Hospital bed density:

0.5 beds/1,000 population (2009)

Drinking water source:

improved:
- *urban*: 93% of population
- *rural*: 92% of population
- *total*: 92% of population

unimproved:
- *urban*: 7% of population
- *rural*: 8% of population

total: 8% of population (2010 est.)

Sanitation facility access:

improved:

urban: 79% of population

rural: 69% of population

total: 74% of population

unimproved:

urban: 21% of population

rural: 31% of population

total: 26% of population (2010 est.)

HIV/AIDS - adult prevalence rate:

less than 0.1% (2009 est.)

country comparison to the world: 155

HIV/AIDS - people living with HIV/AIDS:

8,700 (2009 est.)

country comparison to the world: 104

HIV/AIDS - deaths:

fewer than 200 (2009 est.)

country comparison to the world: 109

Major infectious diseases:

degree of risk: high

food or waterborne diseases: bacterial diarrhea, hepatitis A, and typhoid fever

vectorborne diseases: dengue fever and malaria

water contact disease: leptospirosis (2013)

Obesity - adult prevalence rate:
6.3% (2008)
country comparison to the world: 148

Children under the age of 5 years underweight:
20.7% (2008)
country comparison to the world: 30

Education expenditures:
2.7% of GDP (2009)
country comparison to the world: 151

Literacy:
definition: age 15 and over can read and write
total population: 92.6%
male: 92.5%
female: 92.7% (2000 census)

School life expectancy (primary to tertiary education):
total: 11 years
male: 11 years
female: 12 years (2009)

Unemployment, youth ages 15-24:
total: 17.4%
country comparison to the world: 74
male: 16.2%
female: 19.3% (2009)

Mother's mean age at first birth:
23.1 (2008 est.)

Chapter 3: Government and Key Leaders

Country name:

    conventional long form: Republic of the Philippines

    conventional short form: Philippines

    local long form: Republika ng Pilipinas

    local short form: Pilipinas

Government type:

    republic

Capital:

    name: Manila

    geographic coordinates: 14 36 N, 120 58 E

    time difference: UTC+8 (13 hours ahead of Washington, DC during Standard Time)

Administrative divisions:

    80 provinces and 39 chartered cities

    provinces: Abra, Agusan del Norte, Agusan del Sur, Aklan, Albay, Antique, Apayao, Aurora, Basilan, Bataan, Batanes, Batangas, Biliran, Benguet, Bohol, Bukidnon, Bulacan, Cagayan, Camarines Norte, Camarines Sur, Camiguin, Capiz, Catanduanes, Cavite, Cebu, Compostela, Davao del Norte, Davao del Sur, Davao Oriental, Dinagat Islands, Eastern Samar, Guimaras, Ifugao, Ilocos Norte, Ilocos Sur,

Iloilo, Isabela, Kalinga, Laguna, Lanao del Norte, Lanao del Sur, La Union, Leyte, Maguindanao, Marinduque, Masbate, Mindoro Occidental, Mindoro Oriental, Misamis Occidental, Misamis Oriental, Mountain Province, Negros Occidental, Negros Oriental, North Cotabato, Northern Samar, Nueva Ecija, Nueva Vizcaya, Palawan, Pampanga, Pangasinan, Quezon, Quirino, Rizal, Romblon, Samar, Sarangani, Siquijor, Sorsogon, South Cotabato, Southern Leyte, Sultan Kudarat, Sulu, Surigao del Norte, Surigao del Sur, Tarlac, Tawi-Tawi, Zambales, Zamboanga del Norte, Zamboanga del Sur, Zamboanga Sibugay

chartered cities: Angeles, Antipolo, Bacolod, Baguio, Butuan, Cagayan de Oro, Caloocan, Cebu, Cotabato, Dagupan, Davao, General Santos, Iligan, Iloilo, Lapu-Lapu, Las Pinas, Lucena, Makati, Malabon, Mandaluyong, Mandaue, Manila, Marikina, Muntinlupa, Naga, Navotas, Olongapo, Ormoc, Paranaque, Pasay, Pasig, Puerto Princesa, Quezon, San Juan, Santiago, Tacloban, Taguig, Valenzuela, Zamboanga (2012)

Independence:

12 June 1898 (independence proclaimed from Spain); 4 July 1946 (from the US)

National holiday:
Independence Day, 12 June (1898); note - 12 June 1898 was date of declaration of independence from Spain; 4 July 1946 was date of independence from US

Constitution:
2 February 1987, effective 11 February 1987

Legal system:
mixed legal system of civil, common, Islamic, and customary law

International law organization participation:
accepts compulsory ICJ jurisdiction with reservations; accepts ICCt jurisdiction

Suffrage:
18 years of age; universal

Executive branch:
chief of state: President Benigno AQUINO (since 30 June 2010); Vice President Jejomar BINAY (since 30 June 2010); note - president is both chief of state and head of government
head of government: President Benigno AQUINO (since 30 June 2010)

cabinet: Cabinet appointed by the president with consent of Commission of Appointments

elections: president and vice president elected on separate tickets by popular vote for a single six-year term; election held on 10 May 2010 (next election to be held in May 2016)

election results: Benigno AQUINO elected president; percent of vote - Benigno AQUINO 42.1%, Joseph ESTRADA 26.3%, seven others 31.6%; Jejomar BINAY elected vice president; percent of vote Jejomar BINAY 41.6%, Manuel ROXAS 39.6%, six others 18.8%

Legislative branch:

bicameral Congress or Kongreso consists of the Senate or Senado (24 seats - one-half elected every three years; members elected at large by popular vote to serve six-year terms) and the House of Representatives or Kapulungan Ng Nga Kinatawan (287 seats - 230 members in one tier representing districts and 57 sectoral party-list members in a second tier representing special minorities elected on the basis of one seat for every 2% of the total vote but with each party limited to three seats); a party represented in one tier may not hold seats in the other tier; all House members are elected by popular vote to serve three-year terms

note: the constitution limits the House of Representatives to 250 members; the number of members allowed was increased, however, through legislation when in April 2009 the Philippine Supreme Court ruled that additional party members could sit in the House of Representatives if they received the required number of votes

elections: Senate - elections last held on 13 May 2013 (next to be held in May 2016); House of Representatives - elections last held on 13 May 2013 (next to be held in May 2016)

election results: Senate - percent of vote by party for 2013 election - UNA 26.94%, NP 15.3%, LP 11.32%, NPC 10.15%, LDP 5.38%, PDP-Laban 4.95%, others 9.72%, independents 16.24%; seats by party after 2013 election - UNA 5, NP 5, LP 4, Lakas 2, NPC 2, LDP 1, PDP-Laban 1, PRP 1, independents 3; House of Representatives - percent of vote by party - LP 38.3%, NPC 17.4%, UNA 11.4%, NUP 8.7%, NP 8.5%, Lakas 5.3%, independents 6.0%, others 4.4%; seats by party - LP 110, NPC 43, NUP 24, NP 17,

Lakas 14, UNA 8, independents 6, others 12; party-list 57

Judicial branch:

highest court(s): Supreme Court (consists of a chief justice and 14 associate justices)

judge selection and term of office: justices are appointed by the president on the recommendation of the Judicial and Bar Council, a constitutionally-created, 6-member body that recommends Supreme Court nominees; justices serve until age 70

subordinate courts: Court of Appeals; Sandiganbayan (special court for corruption cases of government officials); Court of Tax Appeals; regional, metropolitan, and municipal trial courts; sharia courts

Political parties and leaders:

Laban ng Demokratikong Pilipino (Struggle of Filipino Democrats) or LDP [Edgardo ANGARA]

Lakas ng EDSA-Christian Muslim Democrats or Lakas-CMD [Manuel "Mar" ROXAS]

Liberal Party or LP [Manuel ROXAS]

Nacionalista Party or NP [Manuel "Manny" VILLAR]

Nationalist People's Coalition or NPC [Frisco SAN JUAN]

PDP-Laban [Aquilino PIMENTEL]

People's Reform Party [Miriam Defensor SANTIAGO]

Puwersa ng Masang Pilipino (Force of the Philippine Masses) or PMP [Joseph ESTRADA]

note: United Nationalist Alliance or [UNA] - PDP-Laban and PMP coalition for the 2013 election

Political pressure groups and leaders:

Black and White Movement [Vicente ROMANO]

Kilosbayan [Jovito SALONGA]

International organization participation:

ADB, APEC, APT, ARF, ASEAN, BIS, CD, CICA (observer), CP, EAS, FAO, G-24, G-77, IAEA, IBRD, ICAO, ICC (national committees), ICRM, IDA, IFAD, IFC, IFRCS, IHO, ILO, IMF, IMO, IMSO, Interpol, IOC, IOM, IPU, ISO, ITSO, ITU, ITUC (NGOs), MIGA, MINUSTAH, NAM, OAS (observer), OPCW, PCA, PIF (partner), UN, UNCTAD, UNDOF, UNESCO, UNHCR, UNIDO, Union Latina, UNISFA, UNMIL, UNMISS, UNMIT, UNMOGIP, UNOCI, UNWTO, UPU, WCO, WFTU (NGOs), WHO, WIPO, WMO, WTO

Diplomatic representation in the US:

chief of mission: Ambassador Jose L. CUISIA Jr.

chancery: 1600 Massachusetts Avenue NW, Washington, DC 20036

telephone: [1] (202) 467-9300

FAX: [1] (202) 467-9417

consulate(s) general: Chicago, Honolulu, Los Angeles, New York, San Francisco, Tamuning (Guam)

Diplomatic representation from the US:

chief of mission: Ambassador Harry K. THOMAS Jr.

embassy: 1201 Roxas Boulevard, Ermita 1000, Manila

mailing address: PSC 500, FPO AP 96515-1000

telephone: [63] (2) 301-2000

FAX: [63] (2) 301-2017

Key Leaders:

Pres.	**Benigno AQUINO III**
Vice Pres.	**Jejomar Cabaiatam BINAY**
Executive Sec.	**Paquito OCHOA, Jr.**
Chief of Staff	**Julia ABAD**
Sec. to the Cabinet	**Jose Rene D. ALMENDRAS**
Sec. of Agrarian	**Virgilio DE LOS**

Reform	**REYES**
Sec. of Agriculture	**Proceso ALCALA**
Sec. of the Budget & Management	**Florencio ABAD**
Sec. of Education, Culture, & Sports	**Armin LUISTRO**, *Rev.*
Sec. of Energy	**Carlos Jericho PETILLA**
Sec. of Environment & Natural Resources	**Ramon PAJE**
Sec. of Finance	**Cesar PURISIMA**
Sec. of Foreign Affairs	**Albert DEL ROSARIO**
Sec. of Health	**Enrique ONA**, *Dr.*
Sec. of Interior & Local Govt.	**Manuel ROXAS II**
Sec. of Justice	**Leila DE LIMA**
Sec. of Labor & Employment	**Rosalinda BALDOZ**

Sec. of National Defense	**Voltaire GAZMIN**
Sec. of Public Works & Highways	**Rogelio L. SINGSON**
Sec. of Science & Technology	**Mario MONTEJO**
Sec. of Social Welfare & Development	**Corazon SOLIMAN**
Sec. of Socioeconomic Planning	**Cayetano PADERANGA**
Sec. of Tourism	**Alberto LIM**
Sec. of Trade & Industry	**Gregory DOMINGO**
Sec. of Transportation & Communications	
National Security Adviser	**Cesar P. GARCIA**, Jr.
Governor, Central	**Amando**

Bank of the Philippines	**TETANGCO**, Jr.
Ambassador to the US	**Jose CUISIA**, Jr.
Permanent Representative to the UN, New York	**Libran N. CABACTULAN**

Flag description:

two equal horizontal bands of blue (top) and red; a white equilateral triangle is based on the hoist side; the center of the triangle displays a yellow sun with eight primary rays; each corner of the triangle contains a small, yellow, five-pointed star; blue stands for peace and justice, red symbolizes courage, the white equal-sided triangle represents equality; the rays recall the first eight provinces that sought independence from Spain, while the stars represent the three major geographical divisions of the country: Luzon, Visayas, and Mindanao; the design of the flag dates to 1897

note: in wartime the flag is flown upside down with the red band at the top

National symbol(s):
> Philippine eagle

National anthem:
> name: "Lupang Hinirang" (Chosen Land)
>
> lyrics/music: Jose PALMA (revised by Felipe PADILLA de Leon)/Julian FELIPE
>
> note: music adopted 1898, original Spanish lyrics adopted 1899, Filipino (Tagalog) lyrics adopted 1956; although the original lyrics were written in Spanish, later English and Filipino versions were created; today, only the Filipino version is used

Chapter 4: Military

Military branches:
 Armed Forces of the Philippines (AFP): Army, Navy (includes Marine Corps), Air Force (2013)

Military service age and obligation:
 17-23 years of age (officers 20-24) for voluntary military service; no conscription; applicants must be single male or female Philippine citizens with either 72 college credit hours (enlisted) or a baccalaureate degree (officers) (2013)

Manpower available for military service:
 males age 16-49: 25,614,135
 females age 16-49: 25,035,061 (2010 est.)

Manpower fit for military service:
 males age 16-49: 20,142,940
 females age 16-49: 21,427,792 (2010 est.)

Manpower reaching militarily significant age annually:
 male: 1,060,319
 female: 1,021,069 (2010 est.)

Military expenditures:
 0.9% of GDP (2005 est.)
 country comparison to the world: 139

Chapter 5: Geography

Location:
Southeastern Asia, archipelago between the Philippine Sea and the South China Sea, east of Vietnam

Geographic coordinates:
13 00 N, 122 00 E

Map references:
Southeast Asia

Area:
total: 300,000 sq km
country comparison to the world: 73
land: 298,170 sq km
water: 1,830 sq km

Area - comparative:
slightly larger than Arizona

Land boundaries:
0 km

Coastline:
36,289 km

Maritime claims:
territorial sea: irregular polygon extending up to 100 nm from coastline as defined by 1898 treaty; since

late 1970s has also claimed polygonal-shaped area in South China Sea up to 285 nm in breadth

exclusive economic zone: 200 nm

continental shelf: to depth of exploitation

Climate:

tropical marine; northeast monsoon (November to April); southwest monsoon (May to October)

Terrain:

mostly mountains with narrow to extensive coastal lowlands

Elevation extremes:

lowest point: Philippine Sea 0 m

highest point: Mount Apo 2,954 m

Natural resources:

timber, petroleum, nickel, cobalt, silver, gold, salt, copper

Land use:

arable land: 18%

permanent crops: 17.33%

other: 64.67% (2011)

Irrigated land:

18,790 sq km (2006)

Total renewable water resources:

479 cu km (2011)

Freshwater withdrawal (domestic/industrial/agricultural):
   total: 81.56 cu km/yr (8%/10%/82%)
   per capita: 859.9 cu m/yr (2009)
Natural hazards:
   astride typhoon belt, usually affected by 15 and struck by five to six cyclonic storms each year; landslides; active volcanoes; destructive earthquakes; tsunamis
   volcanism: significant volcanic activity; Taal (elev. 311 m), which has shown recent unrest and may erupt in the near future, has been deemed a "Decade Volcano" by the International Association of Volcanology and Chemistry of the Earth's Interior, worthy of study due to its explosive history and close proximity to human populations; Mayon (elev. 2,462 m), the country's most active volcano, erupted in 2009 forcing over 33,000 to be evacuated; other historically active volcanoes include Biliran, Babuyan Claro, Bulusan, Camiguin, Camiguin de Babuyanes, Didicas, Iraya, Jolo, Kanlaon, Makaturing, Musuan, Parker, Pinatubo and Ragang
Environment - current issues:
   uncontrolled deforestation especially in watershed areas; soil erosion; air and water pollution in major urban centers; coral reef degradation; increasing

pollution of coastal mangrove swamps that are important fish breeding grounds

Environment - international agreements:

party to: Biodiversity, Climate Change, Climate Change-Kyoto Protocol, Desertification, Endangered Species, Hazardous Wastes, Law of the Sea, Marine Dumping, Ozone Layer Protection, Ship Pollution, Tropical Timber 83, Tropical Timber 94, Wetlands, Whaling

signed, but not ratified: Air Pollution-Persistent Organic Pollutants

Geography - note:

the Philippine archipelago is made up of 7,107 islands; favorably located in relation to many of Southeast Asia's main water bodies: the South China Sea, Philippine Sea, Sulu Sea, Celebes Sea, and Luzon Strait

Chapter 6: Economy

Economy - overview:

Philippine GDP growth, which cooled from 7.6% in 2010 to 3.9% in 2011, expanded to 6.6% in 2012 - meeting the government's targeted 6%-7% growth range. The 2012 expansion partly reflected a rebound from depressed 2011 export and public sector spending levels. The economy has weathered global economic and financial downturns better than its regional peers due to minimal exposure to troubled international securities, lower dependence on exports, relatively resilient domestic consumption, large remittances from four- to five-million overseas Filipino workers, and a rapidly expanding business process outsourcing industry. The current account balance had recorded consecutive surpluses since 2003; international reserves are at record highs; the banking system is stable; and the stock market was Asia's second best-performer in 2012. Efforts to improve tax administration and expenditure management have helped ease the Philippines' tight fiscal situation and reduce high debt levels. The Philippines received several credit rating upgrades on its sovereign debt in 2012, and has had little difficulty tapping domestic and international markets to finance its deficits. Achieving a higher growth path nevertheless remains a pressing challenge. Economic growth in the Philippines averaged 4.5% during the MACAPAGAL-ARROYO administration but poverty worsened during her term. Growth has accelerated under the AQUINO government, but with limited progress thus far in bringing down unemployment, which hovers around 7%, and improving the quality of jobs. Underemployment is nearly 20% and more than 40% of the employed are estimated to be working in the informal sector. The AQUINO administration has been working to boost the budgets for education, health, cash transfers to the poor, and other social spending programs, and is relying on the private sector to help fund major infrastructure projects under its Public-Private Partnership program. Long term challenges include reforming governance and the judicial system, building infrastructure, improving regulatory predictability, and the ease of doing business, attracting higher levels of local and foreign investments. The Philippine Constitution and the other laws continue to restrict foreign ownership in important activities/sectors (such as land ownership and public utilities).

GDP (purchasing power parity):
$431.3 billion (2012 est.)
country comparison to the world: 32
$404.7 billion (2011 est.)
$389.4 billion (2010 est.)
note: data are in 2012 US dollars

GDP (official exchange rate):
$250.4 billion (2012 est.)

GDP - real growth rate:
6.6% (2012 est.)
country comparison to the world: 33
3.9% (2011 est.)
7.6% (2010 est.)

GDP - per capita (PPP):
$4,500 (2012 est.)
country comparison to the world: 165
$4,300 (2011 est.)
$4,200 (2010 est.)
note: data are in 2012 US dollars

GDP - composition by sector:
agriculture: 11.8%

industry: 31.1%

services: 57.1% (2012 est.)

Labor force:

40.42 million (2012 est.)

country comparison to the world: 16

Labor force - by occupation:

agriculture: 32%

industry: 15%

services: 53% (2012 est.)

Unemployment rate:

7% (2012 est.)

country comparison to the world: 78

7% (2011 est.)

Population below poverty line:

26.5% (2009 est.)

Household income or consumption by percentage share:

lowest 10%: 2.6%

highest 10%: 33.6% (2009 est.)

Distribution of family income - Gini index:

44.8 (2009)

country comparison to the world: 42

46.6 (2003)

Investment (gross fixed):

19.4% of GDP (2012 est.)

country comparison to the world: 102

Budget:

revenues: $36.35 billion

expenditures: $42.1 billion (2012 est.)

Taxes and other revenues:

14.5% of GDP (2012 est.)

country comparison to the world: 196

Budget surplus (+) or deficit (-):

-2.3% of GDP (2012 est.)

country comparison to the world: 92

Public debt:

51% of GDP (2012 est.)

country comparison to the world: 64

50.9% of GDP (2011 est.)

note: data cover debt issued by the national government, and excludes debt instruments issued by government entities other than the treasury; the data include treasury debt held by foreign entities; the data exclude debt issued by social security institutions, government-owned and controlled corporations, the Central Bank, and local government units

Inflation rate (consumer prices):

3.1% (2012 est.)

country comparison to the world: 96

4.7% (2011 est.)

Central bank discount rate:

5.3% (31 December 2012 est.)

country comparison to the world: 64

5.6% (31 December 2011 est.)

Commercial bank prime lending rate:

5.68% (31 December 2012 est.)

country comparison to the world: 134

6.66% (31 December 2011 est.)

Stock of narrow money:

$38.93 billion (31 December 2012 est.)

country comparison to the world: 54

$33.97 billion (31 December 2011 est.)

Stock of broad money:

$132.5 billion (31 December 2011 est.)

country comparison to the world: 51

$126 billion (31 December 2010 est.)

Stock of domestic credit:

$129.4 billion (31 December 2012 est.)

country comparison to the world: 49

$112.6 billion (31 December 2011 est.)

Market value of publicly traded shares:

$266.3 billion (31 December 2012)

country comparison to the world: 35

$198.4 billion (31 December 2011)

$202.2 billion (31 December 2010)

Agriculture - products:

sugarcane, coconuts, rice, corn, bananas, cassavas, pineapples, mangoes; pork, eggs, beef; fish

Industries:

electronics assembly, garments, footwear, pharmaceuticals, chemicals, wood products, food processing, petroleum refining, fishing

Industrial production growth rate:

6.8% (2012 est.)

country comparison to the world: 30

Current account balance:

$9.65 billion (2012 est.)

country comparison to the world: 26

$6.988 billion (2011 est.)

Exports:

$46.28 billion (2012 est.)

country comparison to the world: 60

$38.28 billion (2011 est.)

Exports - commodities:

semiconductors and electronic products, transport equipment, garments, copper products, petroleum products, coconut oil, fruits

Exports - partners:
Japan 19%, US 14.2%, China 11.8%, Singapore 9.4%, Hong Kong 9.2%, South Korea 5.5%, Thailand 4.7% (2012)

Imports:
$61.49 billion (2012 est.)
country comparison to the world: 48
$55.25 billion (2011 est.)

Imports - commodities:
electronic products, mineral fuels, machinery and transport equipment, iron and steel, textile fabrics, grains, chemicals, plastic

Imports - partners:
US 11.5%, China 10.8%, Japan 10.4%, South Korea 7.3%, Singapore 7.1%, Thailand 5.6%, Saudi Arabia 5.6%, Indonesia 4.4%, Malaysia 4% (2012)

Reserves of foreign exchange and gold:
$83.83 billion (31 December 2012 est.)
country comparison to the world: 27
$75.3 billion (31 December 2011 est.)

Debt - external:
$74.87 billion (31 December 2012 est.)
country comparison to the world: 54
$76.04 billion (31 December 2011 est.)

Stock of direct foreign investment - at home:
$30.38 billion (31 December 2012 est.)

country comparison to the world: 60

$27.58 billion (31 December 2011 est.)

Stock of direct foreign investment - abroad:
$8.435 billion (31 December 2012 est.)

country comparison to the world: 57

$6.59 billion (31 December 2011 est.)

Exchange rates:

Philippine pesos (PHP) per US dollar:

42.229 (2012 est.)

43.313 (2011 est.)

45.11 (2010 est.)

47.68 (2009)

44.439 (2008)

Fiscal year:

calendar year

Chapter 7: Energy

Electricity - production:
    67.74 billion kWh (2010 est.)
    country comparison to the world: 42

Electricity - consumption:
    64.52 billion kWh (2010 est.)
    country comparison to the world: 40

Electricity - exports:
    0 kWh (2010 est.)
    country comparison to the world: 121

Electricity - imports:
    0 kWh (2010 est.)
    country comparison to the world: 124

Electricity - installed generating capacity:
    16.36 million kW (2010 est.)
    country comparison to the world: 43

Electricity - from fossil fuels:
    66.1% of total installed capacity (2009 est.)
    country comparison to the world: 120

Electricity - from nuclear fuels:
    0% of total installed capacity (2009 est.)
    country comparison to the world: 167

Electricity - from hydroelectric plants:

21.1% of total installed capacity (2009 est.)

country comparison to the world: 88

Electricity - from other renewable sources:

12.8% of total installed capacity (2009 est.)

country comparison to the world: 18

Crude oil - production:

26,640 bbl/day (2011 est.)

country comparison to the world: 69

Crude oil - exports:

28,090 bbl/day (2010 est.)

country comparison to the world: 52

Crude oil - imports:

176,000 bbl/day (2009 est.)

country comparison to the world: 37

Crude oil - proved reserves:

138.5 million bbl (1 January 2013 est.)

country comparison to the world: 70

Refined petroleum products - production:

181,300 bbl/day (2010 est.)

country comparison to the world: 58

Refined petroleum products - consumption:

315,600 bbl/day (2011 est.)

country comparison to the world: 43

Refined petroleum products - exports:

17,810 bbl/day (2010 est.)

country comparison to the world: 75

Refined petroleum products - imports:

147,900 bbl/day (2010 est.)

country comparison to the world: 39

Natural gas - production:

3.91 billion cu m (2012 est.)

country comparison to the world: 53

Natural gas - consumption:

2.86 billion cu m (2010)

country comparison to the world: 74

Natural gas - exports:

0 cu m (2010)

country comparison to the world: 168

Natural gas - imports:

0 cu m (2010)

country comparison to the world: 121

Natural gas - proved reserves:

98.54 billion cu m (1 January 2012 est.)

country comparison to the world: 54

Carbon dioxide emissions from consumption of energy:

85.63 million Mt (2010 est.)

country comparison to the world: 42

Chapter 8: Communications

Telephones - main lines in use:
    3.556 million (2011)
    country comparison to the world: 46

Telephones - mobile cellular:
    94.19 million (2011)
    country comparison to the world: 14

Telephone system:
    general assessment: good international radiotelephone and submarine cable services; domestic and interisland service adequate

    domestic: telecommunications infrastructure includes the following platforms: fixed-line, mobile cellular, cable TV, over-the-air TV, radio and Very Small Aperture Terminal (VSAT), fiber-optic cable, and satellite; mobile-cellular communications now dominate the industry

    international: country code - 63; a series of submarine cables together provide connectivity to Asia, US, the Middle East, and Europe; multiple international gateways (2011)

Broadcast media:

multiple national private TV and radio networks; multi-channel satellite and cable TV systems available; more than 350 TV stations - 4 major TV networks operating nationwide with 1 being government-owned; some 1100 cable TV providers and some 1,200 radio stations broadcasting; the Philippines is scheduled to complete the switch from analog to digital broadcasting by the end of 2015 (2012)

Internet country code:
.ph

Internet hosts:
425,812 (2012)

country comparison to the world: 52

Internet users:
8.278 million (2009)

country comparison to the world: 34

Chapter 9: Transportation

Airports:
    247 (2012)
    country comparison to the world: 25

Airports - with paved runways:
    total: 83
    over 3,047 m: 4
    2,438 to 3,047 m: 8
    1,524 to 2,437 m: 31
    914 to 1,523 m: 31
    under 914 m: 9 (2012)

Airports - with unpaved runways:
    total: 164
    1,524 to 2,437 m: 3
    914 to 1,523 m: 60
    under 914 m: 101 (2012)

Heliports:
    2 (2012)

Pipelines:
    gas 567 km; oil 138 km; refined products 185 km (2013)

Railways:
    total: 995 km

country comparison to the world: 88

narrow gauge: 995 km 1.067-m gauge (484 km are in operation) (2010)

Roadways:

total: 213,151 km

country comparison to the world: 23

paved: 54,481 km

unpaved: 158,670 km (2009)

Waterways:

3,219 km (limited to vessels with draft less than 1.5 m) (2011)

country comparison to the world: 31

Merchant marine:

total: 446

country comparison to the world: 23

by type: bulk carrier 76, cargo 152, carrier 12, chemical tanker 27, container 17, liquefied gas 5, passenger 7, passenger/cargo 65, petroleum tanker 44, refrigerated cargo 20, roll on/roll off 11, vehicle carrier 10

foreign-owned: 159 (Bermuda 47, China 4, Denmark 2, Germany 2, Greece 5, Japan 77, Malaysia 1, Netherlands 17, Singapore 1, South Korea 1, Taiwan 1, UAE 1) registered in other countries: 7 (Cyprus 1, Panama 5, unknown 1) (2010)

Ports and terminals:

Batangas, Cagayan de Oro, Cebu, Davao, Liman, Manila

Transportation - note:

the International Maritime Bureau reports the territorial and offshore waters in the South China Sea as high risk for piracy and armed robbery against ships; numerous commercial vessels have been attacked and hijacked both at anchor and while underway; hijacked vessels are often disguised and cargo diverted to ports in East Asia; crews have been murdered or cast adrift

Chapter 10: Transnational Issues

Disputes - international:

Philippines claims sovereignty over Scarborough Reef (also claimed by China together with Taiwan) and over certain of the Spratly Islands, known locally as the Kalayaan (Freedom) Islands, also claimed by China, Malaysia, Taiwan, and Vietnam; the 2002 "Declaration on the Conduct of Parties in the South China Sea," has eased tensions in the Spratly Islands but falls short of a legally binding "code of conduct" desired by several of the disputants; in March 2005, the national oil companies of China, the Philippines, and Vietnam signed a joint accord to conduct marine seismic activities in the Spratly Islands; Philippines retains a dormant claim to Malaysia's Sabah State in northern Borneo based on the Sultanate of Sulu's granting the Philippines Government power of attorney to pursue a sovereignty claim on his behalf; maritime delimitation negotiations continue with Palau

Refugees and internally displaced persons:

IDPs: at least 843,000 (government troops fighting the Moro Islamic Liberation Front, the Abu Sayyaf

Group, and the New People's Army; clan feuds; natural disasters (December 2012 Typhoon Bopha)) (2013)

Illicit drugs:
domestic methamphetamine production has been a growing problem in recent years despite government crackdowns; major consumer of amphetamines; longstanding marijuana producer mainly in rural areas where Manila's control is limited

Map of the Philippines

Other Key Facts™ Titles

Key Facts on Syria

Key Facts on China

Key Facts on Qatar

Key Facts on India

Key Facts on Germany

Key Facts on Argentina

Key Facts on Russia

Key Facts on North Korea

Key Facts on Brazil

Key Facts on Italy

Key Facts on the United Arab Emirates

Key Facts on the European Union

Key Facts on Pakistan

Key Facts on Saudi Arabia

Key Facts on Cyprus

Key Facts on Iran

Key Facts on Afghanistan

Key Facts on Iraq

Key Facts on Indonesia

Key Facts on South Korea

Key Facts on France

Key Facts on the United Kingdom

Key Facts on Egypt

Key Facts on Israel

Key Facts on Mexico

Key Facts on the United States of America

Key Facts on Turkey

Key Facts on South Africa

Key Facts on Greece

Key Facts on Japan

Key Facts on Malaysia

Key Facts on Vietnam

Key Facts on Hong Kong

Key Facts on Jordan

Key Facts on Australia

Key Facts on Venezuela

Key Facts on Canada

Key Facts on Burma (Myanmar)

Key Facts on Myanmar (Burma)

Key Facts on Singapore

Key Facts on Ireland

All Key Facts™ Titles are Available at

www.Amazon.com

THE INTERNATIONALIST®

2013

WWW.INTERNATIONALIST.COM

www.ingramcontent.com/pod-product-compliance
Lightning Source LLC
Chambersburg PA
CBHW071642170526
45166CB00003B/1400